Magic

HANDBOOK

MAGIC WITH NUMBERS

Jon Tremaine

QEB Publishing

Editor: Michael Downey
Designer: Louise Downey
Illustrator: Mark Turner for
          Beehive Illustrations

Picture credits
Anikó Ungár 13
Corbis: Bettmann/CORBIS 16
Getty Images: 7, Barcroft Media via Getty Images 11
Shutterstock: Berislav Kovacevic 21

Copyright © QEB Publishing, Inc. 2010

Published in the United States by
QEB Publishing, Inc.
3 Wrigley, Suite A
Irvine, CA 92618

www.qed-publishing.co.uk

A CIP record for this book is available from the
Library of Congress.

ISBN 978 1 59566 945 2

Printed in China

Contents

Magic with numbers

 Tricks and puzzles using numbers are fun to do. The best thing of all is that they always work! This is because there are some magical rules that apply to numbers. These make it possible for you to do what appear to be really difficult sums, and get the right answer. Your friends will be impressed!

② **Difficulty rating**

The tricks get harder throughout the book, so each trick has been given a rating. One is the easiest and five is the hardest. The most difficult tricks will take a bit of practice to get right, but the results will be worth it!

① **Preparation**

Sometimes you may need to prepare part of the trick before you start your performance.

Putting on a show

There is much more to doing these tricks than writing lots of numbers on a piece of paper. To make it more exciting for your audience, you must do a little bit of acting, too. In other words, you could pretend that you don't know if the trick or puzzle will work or not. Pretend to be surprised when it does—which is always!

Special number

The number 1089 is magical. Ask you friend to do a few sums, and the answer will be 1089! Your friend will think you have special powers when you predict the answer!

① **Preparation**

• Write the number 1089 on one side of the piece of paper.

1089

Floating light bulb

Harry Blackstone, Jnr (1934 - 1997) performed a brilliant trick with a light bulb. First he made the bulb light up in his hand. Then, the bulb floated around the stage, still lit. It then floated over the heads of the audience before returning to the magician's hand. With a wave of his hand, the lighted bulb finally disappeared!

⑥

Props needed...

The props you will need throughout the book.

- 200 coins
- Battery
- Bracelet
- Button
- Cardboard
- Cardboard box
- Chewing gum
- Dice
- Domino set

- Envelopes
- Glass bowl
- Key
- Marker pen
- Matchstick
- Paper
- Pencil
- Playing cards
- Pocket calculator
- Ring

- Safety pin
- Scissors
- Small notebook
- Sticky tape

④ **Stages and illustrations**

Step-by-step instructions, as well as illustrations, will guide you through each trick.

⑤ **Top Tip!**

Hints and tips help you to perform the tricks better!

⑥ **Famous magicians and illusions**

Find out who are the most exciting and skillful magicians, and what amazing feats they have performed.

⑦ **Logic puzzle**

Challenge your friends to work out a tricky puzzle!

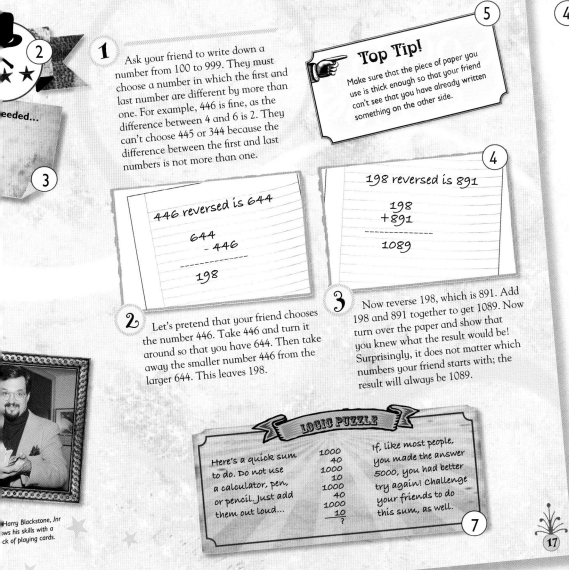

1 Ask your friend to write down a number from 100 to 999. They must choose a number in which the first and last number are different by more than one. For example, 446 is fine, as the difference between 4 and 6 is 2. They can't choose 445 or 344 because the difference between the first and last numbers is not more than one.

Top Tip! Make sure that the piece of paper you use is thick enough so that your friend can't see that you have already written something on the other side.

446 reversed is 644

644
− 446
‾‾‾‾‾‾‾
198

198 reversed is 891

198
+891
‾‾‾‾‾‾‾
1089

2 Let's pretend that your friend chooses the number 446. Take 446 and turn it around so that you have 644. Then take away the smaller number 446 from the larger 644. This leaves 198.

3 Now reverse 198, which is 891. Add 198 and 891 together to get 1089. Now turn over the paper and show that you knew what the result would be! Surprisingly, it does not matter which numbers your friend starts with; the result will always be 1089.

LOGIC PUZZLE

Here's a quick sum to do. Do not use a calculator, pen, or pencil. Just add them out loud...

1000
40
1000
10
1000
40
1000
10
‾‾‾
?

If, like most people, you made the answer 5000, you had better try again! Challenge your friends to do this sum, as well.

17

Harry Blackstone, Jnr ...ws his skills with a ...ck of playing cards.

5

The 3½ of Clubs

With just a playing card, an envelope, and a die, you can ask your friend to give you a number and predict it correctly.

Preparation

• Take the black marker pen and write a "½" after each number 3 on the 3 of Clubs card. Also draw the extra half-club symbol.

• Insert the card into the envelope. Put the envelope and the die onto a table when you start the trick.

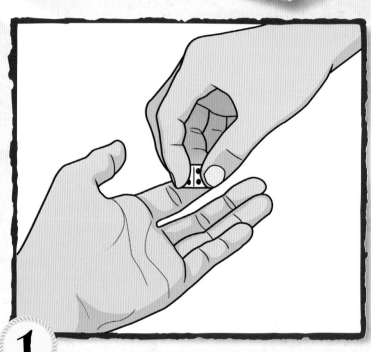

1

Say to your friend, "Inside this small envelope is a playing card. The number on this hidden card is the same as the one you are about to give me!" Then give your friend the die.

Explanation!

The answer will always be 3½, because the opposite sides of a die always total seven—1 + 6 = 7, 2 + 5 = 7, and 3 + 4 = 7.

2 Say, "When my back is turned, I want you to roll the die. When it stops, add the number on the top of the die to the number on the bottom. Then divide this total by two." After a short pause, add, "The number of the playing card in the envelope will be the same as your total."

3 "Have you done that? What was your final total?" Your friend will say, "3½" and laugh, because they will think that they have caught you out. You should pretend to be upset. Then, slowly, pull out the 3½ of Clubs from the envelope to show that you were right after all!

▼ Sorcar performs his grisly illusion in London in 1956. Don't worry! It was an illusion—his female assistant was not harmed!

Televized sensation

The great Indian magician P. C. Sorcar (1913–1971) caused a sensation in Britain when he performed an illusion live on television. His female assistant was laid on a table and a huge, rotating circular saw was lowered onto her middle. It appeared to slice her in two! Unfortunately, the live television broadcast ran out of time at this point. Millions of worried viewers were left wondering what had happened to her!

Domino trick

How can you predict which dominoes will be at the two ends of a line of dominoes? Especially as you won't be in the room when your friend lays them out!

Props needed...
* Domino set
* Envelope
* Paper and pencil

Preparation

• Secretly take one of the dominoes. For example, it could be a 6-1. Write on a piece of paper "I predict that the two end numbers will be a one and a six".

• Put the paper in an envelope and seal it. Place the envelope on a table with the set of dominoes before you start.

I predict that the two end numbers will be a one and a six.

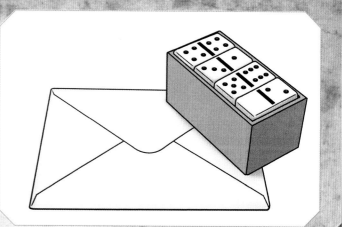

1 Put the dominoes out on a table so that they are all face up. Tell your friend to start matching up the dominoes in the same way as they would when playing a game of dominoes. That is, put a five-dots pattern against another five-dots pattern, and so on.

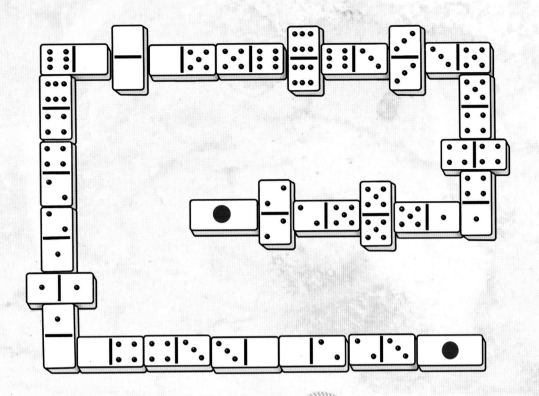

2

Before your friend starts joining the dominoes together, tell them that you will leave the room for a short while. Before you go, tell them that they should leave the dominoes at each end of the line face down. That way, when you come back into the room you won't be able to see what they are.

3

When you return, pretend to look at the dominoes on the table carefully. Then tell your friend the numbers on the face-down dominoes. In this example, they will be 3–1 and 2–6.

☞ Top Tip!

You can repeat the trick by secretly replacing the domino that you had taken and stealing another one in its place! In this trick, the two end numbers in the domino spread will always be the same as the numbers on the domino you took away. It's magic!

4

Now ask your friend to open the envelope and read out your prediction. This will, of course, be correct!

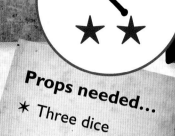

Top and bottom

This is a great mind-reading trick that is based on a simple fact. That is, when added together, the top and bottom numbers of a dice always total seven.

Props needed...
* Three dice

1 Ask your friend to stack the three dice, one on top of another. Before they do this, turn your back to your friend so that you can't see the dice.

2 Give your friend enough time to make the stack. Then turn around for a split second and say, "Have you done that yet?" Immediately turn your head away again to make it seem that you did not see the dice. In this split second, look at the number at the top of the dice pile. Let's say it is a three.

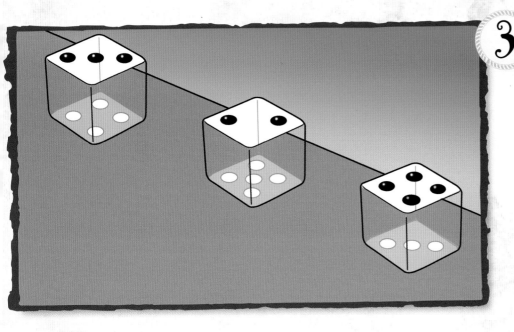

3 Then say, "There are five sides of the dice that you can't see – the one at the bottom and the four sides sandwiched between the dice. Look at these sides of the dice and add their numbers together. Don't say the total out loud; just think of the total."

Wait for a few seconds, then say, "You are thinking of the number 18." If the top number was three, you will be right!

Explanation!

When added up, the top and bottom sides of a dice always total seven. Therefore, the top and bottom sides of three dice will always total 21. You just have to subtract the number that you secretly glimpsed from 21 to arrive at the correct answer.

Indian rope trick

Magician Howard Thurston (1869-1936), from Ohio in the United States, had the largest traveling magic show of his time. It took a train more than ten cars long to transport his props. Thurston featured the famous Indian rope trick. A rope is thrown up into the air, and stays there. A little boy then climbs to the top of a rope and vanishes!

◄ *The Indian rope trick was first performed in India in the 1800s.*

Speedy math

It is simple to do a difficult sum—you just have to know the secret formula. Your friends will think that you are a math genius when you show them this numbers trick!

Props needed...
* Pencil
* Paper

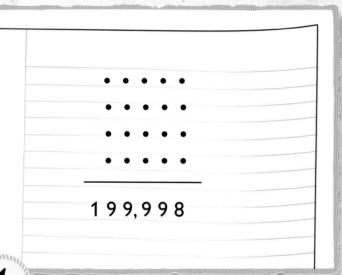

```
· · · · ·
· · · · ·
· · · · ·
· · · · ·
_____
  199,998
```

```
  76045
· · · · ·
  29283
· · · · ·
_____
  199,998
```

1 Draw four rows of five dots on a piece of paper. Then draw a line beneath the dots to show that it is a sum. Fill in 199,998 under the line as the total.

2 Ask your friends to fill in the first and third lines with any numbers that they wish. It is their choice. Let's suppose that they wrote 76,045 and 29,283.

Explanation!

How do you know what numbers to use? All you do is write a number that, when added to the number above, will add up to nine. The first number in the top line is a seven, so under it you put a two. Next is a six, so you put a three, and so on. You also use this method with the fourth row. Easy!

3 Say that you will fill in the gaps with numbers to make the total correct. You will make things more difficult for yourself by starting from the left side—not the right side, which is the normal way of doing sums. You will do this in only 10 seconds!

```
  76045
  23954
  29283
  70716
───────────
 199,998
```

4 After you have filled in your numbers, the sum looks like this. Your sum, of course, is correct.

Starting young

Hungary's most famous magician, Anikó Ungár, has performed her stunning magic shows all over the world. These have earned her many important prizes. After studying textile design at an early age, Anikó Ungár changed direction and went on to build a career as a magician. Encouraged by her father, who was an amateur magician, she learned her first tricks at the age of 13.

▶ Anikó Ungár uses a wide variety of props during her stunning magic shows.

Always 34

Props needed...
* Pencil
* Paper

This mathematical trick is totally baffling, but it works every time! It is easy to do. All you need is a pencil and a piece of paper on which you write the numbers 1 to 16.

Preparation

• Secretly write the number 34 on the back of the piece of paper.

34

1

1	2	3	4
5	6	7	8
9	10	11	12
13	14	15	16

Write the numbers 1 to 16 on the blank side of the piece of paper. Use the pattern shown here.

2

1	2	3	4
5	6	7	8
9	10	11	12
13	14	15	16

Ask your friend to say a number from 1 to 16. Let's pretend they choose number 11. Draw a circle around 11 and then the two lines through it, as shown.

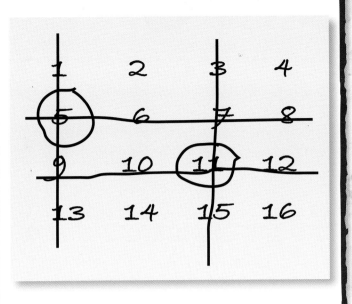

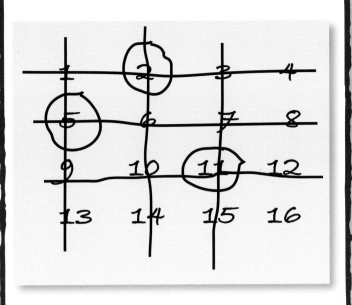

3 Show your friend the piece of paper. Ask them to choose another number that does not have a line through it. Let's assume they say 5. Cross this out both ways as you did with 11.

4 Ask your friend to choose another number that has not been crossed through. This time, let's pretend they say 2. Draw lines through this number, as you did before.

5 Only the number 16 has not been struck through. Ask your friend to add 16 to the three numbers they have already chosen. This is the sum:

16 + 11 + 5 + 2 = 34

Turn over the paper and show that you have already written 34!

Top Tip!
This trick will work every time, no matter which numbers are chosen. The total will always be 34.

LOGIC PUZZLE

Question: Two rows of coins are laid out as shown. One row contains five coins; the other, four coins. By moving only one coin, how can you end up with two rows, each four coins long?

O O O O O
O
O
O

Answer: Put two coins at the corner point, one on top of the other!

O O O O
O
O
O

Special number

The number 1089 is magical. Ask your friend to do a few sums, and the answer will be 1089! Your friend will think you have special powers when you predict the answer!

Props needed...
* Paper
* Pencil

Preparation

• Write the number 1089 on one side of the piece of paper.

1089

Floating light bulb

Harry Blackstone, Jnr. (1934–1997) performed a brilliant trick with a light bulb. First he made the bulb light up in his hand. Then, the bulb floated around the stage, still lit. It then floated over the heads of the audience before returning to the magician's hand. With a wave of his hand, the lighted bulb finally disappeared!

▲ Magician Harry Blackstone, Jnr. shows his skills with a pack of playing cards.

1

Ask your friend to write down a number from 100 to 999. They must choose a number in which the first and last number are different by more than one. For example, 446 is fine, as the difference between 4 and 6 is 2. They can't choose 445 or 344, because the difference between the first and last numbers is not more than one.

446 reversed is 644

```
  644
- 446
-------------
  198
```

198 reversed is 891

```
  198
+ 891
-------------
 1089
```

2

Let's pretend that your friend chooses the number 446. Take 446 and turn it around so that you have 644. Then take away the smaller number 446 from the larger 644. This leaves 198.

3

Now reverse 198, which is 891. Add 198 and 891 together to get 1089. Now turn over the paper and show that you knew what the result would be! Surprisingly, it does not matter which numbers your friend starts with, the result will always be 1089.

LOGIC PUZZLE

Here's a quick sum to do. Do not use a calculator, pen, or pencil. Just add them out loud...

```
 1000
   40
 1000
   10
 1000
   40
 1000
   10
------
    ?
```

If, like most people, you made the answer 5000, you had better try again! Challenge your friends to do this sum, as well.

Pick a picture

★ ★ ★

Ask your friend to think about just one object from a piece of cardboard containing more than 30 pictures. Then tell them which object they were thinking about!

Props needed...
* Cardboard
* Scissors

Preparation

• Photocopy these six charts onto thick paper or cardboard and cut out each one. There is one large card and five smaller ones.

1 Show your friend the large card with 31 pictures on it. Ask your friend to think about just one of the objects.

2 Once your friend has picked one of the objects, give them the five smaller cards. Ask them to look at each smaller card carefully and give you back the cards that have a picture of the object that they are thinking about.

3 As soon as they have done this, you can tell which object they chose!

4 How? Easy! Add together the grey numbers that appear in the top left-hand picture of each of the smaller cards that your friend gives you back. Taking this total, look at the big chart and find the object that lies in the square with that number. This will be the object that your friend thought about. It works every time!

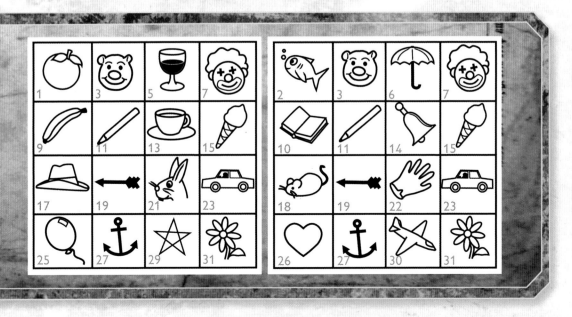

Magic 115 trick

Props needed...
* Pocket calculator

By using simple mathematics—and the magic number 115—you can tell a person the number that they are thinking about as well as their age!

1

It is best to do this trick with an adult whose age you do not know. Ask them to do the following:

– Enter their age into the calculator
– Multiply it by two
– Add five
– Multiply by 50
– Subtract 365
– Think of any number under 100 and add that to the total

The person then tells you the grand total, and you tell them their age and the number they had thought about! How can you possibly do this?

Age		44
x 2	=	88
+ 5	=	93
x 50	=	4650
- 365	=	4285
+ 27	=	4312

2

Let's say that their age is 44 and the number they thought about was 27. The total they show you is 4312. This is where the magic number 115 is used! Secretly, add 115 to their total.

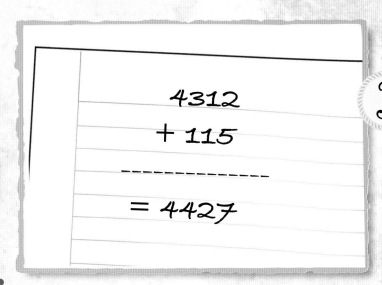

```
    4312
  + 115
  --------------
  = 4427
```

3

The first two digits give us their age, and the second two give us the number they thought about. Easy!

To prove that it works every time,
here are two more examples:

Age		56
x 2	=	112
+ 5	=	117
x 50	=	5850
- 365	=	5485
+ 99	=	5584
+ 115	=	5699

A 56-year-old thinks of number 99.

Age		13
x 2	=	26
+ 5	=	31
x 50	=	1550
- 365	=	1185
+ 24	=	1209
+ 115	=	1324

A 13-year-old thinks of number 24.

X-ray eyes

Kuda Bux (1906–1981) had an amazing act. While on stage, his eyes were covered with soft dough, aluminum foil, gauze and bandages, and his head wrapped in strips of cloth. He then amazed his audience by reading from books put in front of him. In August 1938 a 1-metre-deep pit was dug in a car park in New York. It was filled with charcoal and logs and set alight. Kuda Bux walked barefoot through the pit—twice!

▶ How could Kuda Bux walk through the fiery pit? Afterwards his feet were not even warm!

PEARSON'S WEEKLY

2D
SEPT. 14,
1935
No. 2355

HE WILL WALK THROUGH FIRE

Passport to mystery

Your friend multiplies your passport number by a number they choose between 1 and 7. You, however, have already written down the total!

Props needed...
* Small notebook
* Long strip of paper
* Pencil
* Sticky tape
* Pocket calculator

Preparation

1. Write the number 142857 on the long slip of paper, with the digits spaced as shown.

$$1 \quad 4 \quad 2 \quad 8 \quad 5 \quad 7$$

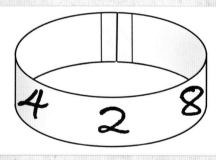

The number 142857 is unusual. This is because if you multiply it by 2, 3, 4, 5, or 6, the numbers that appear in the answer are the same. They can be read clockwise around the circle, starting at a different digit.

2. Join the two ends of the strip together with sticky tape. Flatten the circle and put it in your pocket.

$142857 \times 2 = 285714$—to read the answer, start at number 2

3. Write "Passport number 142857" in your notebook. You will pretend that this is your passport number. Put the notebook in your pocket.

Passport number 142857

$142857 \times 3 = 428571$—to read the answer, start at number 4

$142857 \times 4 = 571428$—to read the answer, start at number 5

$142857 \times 5 = 714285$—to read the answer, start at number 7

$142857 \times 6 = 857142$—to read the answer, start at number 8

1 Start by giving the calculator to your friend. Then take the notebook and strip of paper out of your pocket.

2 Say that you will try an experiment with your passport number. Open the notebook and ask your friend to enter the number into the calculator as you read it out.

3 Your friend enters the number 142857 into the calculator.

4 Ask them to think of a number between 1 and 7 and say it out loud. Let's pretend they say "4."

5 Ask your friend to multiply your passport number by 4.

6 As quickly as you can, tear the strip so that the number 5 becomes the first number on the left-hand side of your strip. Compare your strip to the calculator. The numbers are the same!

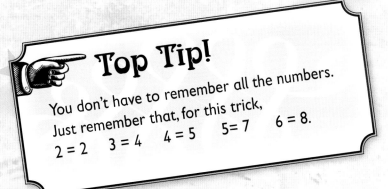

Top Tip!

You don't have to remember all the numbers. Just remember that, for this trick,

2 = 2   3 = 4   4 = 5   5 = 7   6 = 8.

Piggy bank

Thshis great trick shows how devious magicians can be! Your friend holds a number of coins hidden in their hands. You show that you know exactly how many coins they are holding.

Props needed...
* 200 coins
* Glass bowl
* Paper
* Pencil

Preparation

• Place the 200 coins into a clear glass bowl.

1

Ask your friend to grab a handful of coins from the glass bowl. Then, you grab a handful of coins. It is important that you pick up more coins than your friend.

2 Say to your friend, "In a moment. we will turn our backs and count the number of coins we are holding. Please do not tell me how many coins you have—just remember the total." You also count your coins. Do not tell your friend how many coins you have.

3 Let's assume that you have picked up 33 coins. Subtract 3 from this total, giving you 30.

Top Tip!

You could have deducted any small number from your total at the start: say, 5. Then your statement would have been, "I have the same number of coins as you. I will have 5 over and enough left to make your total up to 28."

4 Say to your friend, "I'm going to make three statements, all of which are true."
1. "I will match the number of coins you have."
2. "I will have three coins extra."
3. "I will have enough coins left to take your total up to 30 coins."

"So, how many coins have you got?"

5 They say they have 19 coins. Now repeat each statement and give your friend the correct number of coins.
"I have the same number of coins as you." Put 19 coins back into the glass bowl from your coins.
"I will have three coins extra." Count three more coins back into the bowl.
"I will have enough coins left to take your total up to 30 coins." Count the remaining 11 coins back into the bowl to make 30 coins!

Him	You
19	33
+ 11	− 3
	30
= 30	− 19
	= 11

The "Q" trick

Props needed...
* Pack of playing cards

Your friend silently looks at a playing card, which is somewhere in a spread of cards. You do not know what card this is, but you still find it!

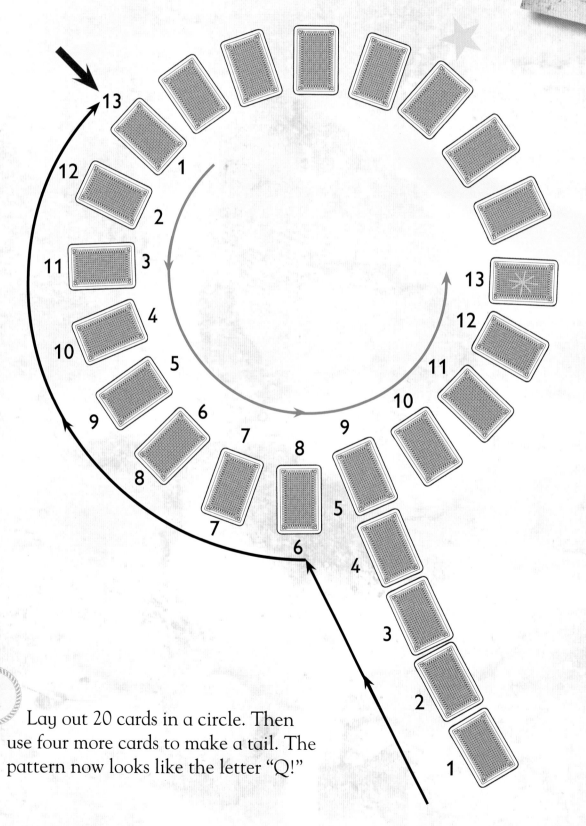

1

Lay out 20 cards in a circle. Then use four more cards to make a tail. The pattern now looks like the letter "Q!"

2

Ask your friend to think of a number between 5 and 20. Starting with card 1 at the end of the tail, they should then silently count the cards until they reach the number they are thinking about. They must move around the circle in a clockwise direction. In other words, using the numbers on the outside of the circle in the diagram.

3

When they reach the card with the number they were thinking about, they should make this card the new card 1. If they were thinking of the number 13, card 13 is now the new card 1—this is marked with a red arrow in the diagram. Tell them again that they must do all this silently.

4

From the new card 1, your friend now silently counts backward, or counterclockwise, by the same number of cards. This time, they keep going around the circle as shown by the blue arrow—they do not go down the tail. Tell them that, when they reach the new card, they must look at and think about the card. They should not tell you what the card is.

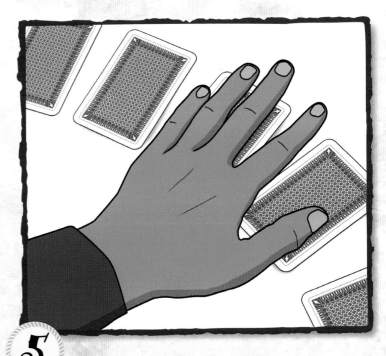

5

Now pass your hand over all the cards as if trying to pick up a vibration from them. Finally, you pick up the correct card and hand it to your friend!

How do you do this? The answer lies in the tail of the Q. There are five cards in the tail, so your friend's card will be the fifth card counting counterclockwise from the top of the tail. It does not matter what number they think about; they will always arrive at the same position. Try it for yourself and see!

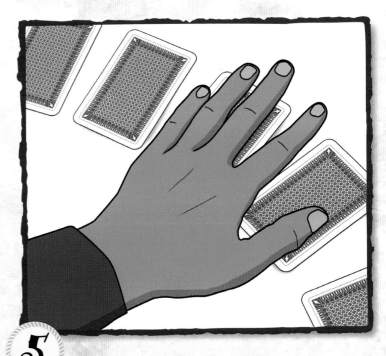
TOP TIP
If you want to repeat the trick, just put a few more cards in the tail. Your friend's final position will then be slightly different.

Matching halves

Your friend tells you how to divide up five playing cards that you have cut in half. You manage to match up the half-cards, even though they are placed face down on the table.

Props needed...

* Any five playing cards from an old pack

Preparation

• Cut each card in half and lay them out on the table as shown.

Top Tip!

You could use picture postcards instead of playing cards. Or, you could ask five friends to write their names across blank visiting cards, cut them in half, and then do the trick.

1 Gather up the two rows of cards without disturbing their order. Then place one pile on top of the other.

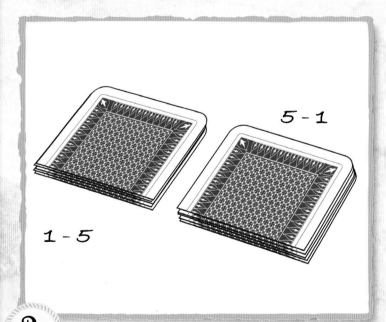

5 - 1

1 - 5

2 Hold the pile of ten half-cards face down in your left hand. Then deal five half-cards, one at a time, onto the table in a pile. You have now reversed the order of these five. Without reversing them, put the other five cards on the table next to these.

3

Say to your friend, "This trick uses the phrase 'Last Two Cards Match.' I am going to spell out the phrase 'Last Two Cards Match' using these pieces of card. You are going to tell me exactly what to do and you must make sure that I obey all your instructions. Let's start."

4

"Which of the two piles would you like me to start with?" When your friend points to a pile, you pick it up. "Our first word is 'Last.' I remove one half-card from the top of this pile and take it to the bottom of the pile to represent the letter 'L.'" While you are talking, make this move.

5

"Now we must move a half-card for the next letter, 'A.' Shall I use the pile that I'm holding or the other pile?" If your friend says the pile that you are holding, just move a card, as before. Use the other pile if they ask for this. Do the same for the letters "S" and "T," obeying your friend's instructions. Now take the top card from each pile and place both on one side, without showing their faces.

6

Do the same for the words "Two," "Cards," and "Match." Remember to put aside the next two top half-cards when you finish spelling each word. You are now left with two half-cards.

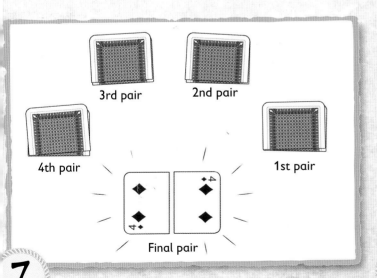

3rd pair   2nd pair

4th pair   1st pair

Final pair

7

Turn them over to show that the last two cards do match! Your friend will think the trick is over, but you have a surprise for them.

8

Turn the other four sets of pairs face up. Wow—they all match up, too!

Pieces of eight

Throw eight small objects into a box. Ask your friend to think of one, without telling you what it is. Then take them out, one by one, until you know you are holding the one your friend chose!

Props needed...
* Key
* Ring
* Match
* Button
* Battery
* Bracelet
* Safety pin
* Chewing gum
* Cardboard box

Preparation

• Each of the objects that you use has a different number of letters in its name. You can use other items, but make sure they have the right number of letters.

chewing gum	10 letters
safety pin	9 letters
bracelet	8 letters
battery	7 letters
button	6 letters
match	5 letters
ring	4 letters
key	3 letters

• Make sure the objects are small enough for each to be hidden in a clenched hand.

• Remember how many letters there are in the name of each object.

1 Put all eight objects on the table together with the box. Pick up the objects in any order and put them in the box. As you do so, name each one out loud. For example, say "match," "bracelet," and so on.

2 Ask a friend to look into the box. They should silently choose one of the objects and think about it.

4 Put your hand in the box and take out any object, hidden in your clenched hand. Wait a few seconds, then put the object back in the box. Then take out another one.

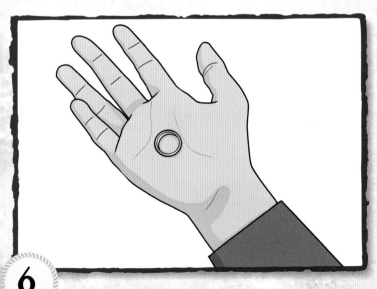

6 If not, continue. Take out the ring (four letters). If they are thinking of the ring, they will shout, "Stop"—there is the ring in your hand!

3 Explain that you will now lift objects out of the box, one at a time. The object will be hidden in your hand. Each time you take an object out, your friend must silently think about one letter of the name of their chosen object. When they reach the last letter of the name, they must say, "Stop."

5 Put the object back into the box after a few seconds. This time, take out the key. If your friend is thinking of the key (three letters), they will now shout "Stop!" Ask them to tell you which object they were thinking about. They say, "The key". You open your hand and, to their amazement, there is the key!

7 Continue taking out the object with the next largest number of letters in its name. Do this until your friend shouts, "Stop." Whenever you open your hand, the correct object will be in it!

Math puzzle

How can you get two different answers for the same sum? It depends on how you approach the problem!

1. Three friends reach a hotel late at night, but only one room is available. They decide to share the room.

2. The room costs $30 for the night, so each person agrees to pay $10.

3. They go up to the room. After a while, there is a knock on the door. It is the hotel bellhop, who tells them that, as it is Wednesday night, the room is only $25, not $30. The bellhop gives them back $5.

4. The friends are so impressed with the honesty of the bellhop that they give him a $2 tip and keep $1 each.

These are the sums.

	Friend one	Friend two	Friend three
Cost of room	$10	$10	$10
Refund	$1	$1	$1

Total cost each	$9	$9	$9
The tip to the porter was £2			
So that is $9 + $9 + $9 + $2, which is $29!			

What has happened to the other $1? Let's start again!

1. With the $5 refund, the friends paid $25 for the room, not $30.

2. So it cost each friend one third of $25, which is $8.33.

3. They decided to tip the bellhop $2 and each keep $1.

4. The $5 was their money in the first place and has got nothing to do with the cost of the room. Therefore, there was no vanishing $1!